I WANT TO SEE
HIS FACE

TERE DE LA ROSA

Written and prepared by: Tere De la Rosa

*© 2024 DLR Legacy Inc.
Bradenton, FL 34212*

*Cover Design: Briaquel Alfaro
Cover Drawing: Brooke Stefanelli
Edited by: Rhonda Vitanza & Rosa Rivera*

ISBN: 978-1-7361467-3-6

All rights reserved. No portion of this publication may be reproduced, stored in an electronic system, or transmitted in any form or by any means, electronic, mechanical, photocopy, recording, or otherwise, without the prior permission of DLR Legacy Inc. Brief quotations may be used.

*Unless otherwise indicated, all Scripture quotations are taken from the following translations:
King James Version (KJV)
New International Version (NIV)
Amplified Bible (AMP)
New Living Translation (NLT)*

For verses not specifically mentioned, the default reference is the King James Version.

Printed in the United States of America

*The smoke of the incense,
together with the prayers of God's people,
went up before God from the angel's hand.
Revelation 8:4 (NIV)*

*For the earth will be filled
with the knowledge of the glory of the Lord
as the waters cover the sea.
Habakkuk 2:14 (NIV)*

Index

Foreword 1

Introduction 5

Seek His Face 9

Into His Gates 11

Pray Following The Model Given By The Lord 15

Thy Kingdom Come 35

Thy Will Be Done, ... 39

Give Us Day By Day Our Daily Bread 42

And Forgive Us Our Sins 47

For we also Forgive Every one 50

And Lead Us Not Into Temptation 52

But Deliver Us From Evil 53

Pray With Songs And Psalms 55

Pray without ceasing

1 Thessalonians 5:17 (KJV)

Foreword

I first met Tere De la Rosa in 2006 as we shared many responsibilities in ministry together for our church organization. Her anointing was evident from our first encounter. Throughout our years of friendship, I have watched as the Lord has used her locally, nationally, and internationally to share His gospel.

Tere excels in the area of Communications. Once a television personality in the Dominican Republic, she now uses her talents for God's Kingdom. One of her many talents is in the area of writing. Her burden to help others is the catalyst for all of her books and articles, which include: a compilation of Spanish music; Bajo la Sombra del Altísimo (Under The Shadow Of The Most High); La Madre del Hijo Prodigo (The Mother of The Prodigal), a book to encourage and help family members of prodigals; many published articles and UPCI Ladies website contributions, and most recently this prayer guide. She has also successfully translated several books and articles from English to Spanish. In addition,

Tere also has a podcast entitled "Levántate y Resplandece" (Arise and Shine), and a YouTube Channel that transmit her devotional "De Gloria en Gloria (From Glory To Glory) which also reaches thousands monthly. She is a highly sought after speaker for ladies conferences in the US and abroad. Tere is a licensed minister with the United Pentecostal Church, International.

I'm confident this prayer guide will help you, as it has helped me. Carry it in your bible or in your car for those lunchtimes dedicated to and spent with God. Share them with your family members and keep a few handy to open up a conversation with others about the Lord. I pray Tere's ministry is a blessing to you, and I feel honored to write this forward for her newest project.

Rev. Rhonda Vitanza

Praise the Lord!

Praise God in his sanctuary;
praise him in his mighty heavens.
Praise him for his acts of power;
praise him for his surpassing greatness.
Praise him with the sounding of the trumpet,
praise him with the harp and lyre,
praise him with timbrel and dancing,
praise him with the strings and pipe,
praise him with the clash of cymbals,
praise him with resounding cymbals.
Let everything that has breath praise the Lord.
Praise the Lord.
Psalm 150 (NIV)

Pray always

Introduction

Prayer is communication with the Almighty God, whom we have the privilege of knowing not only by his attributes, but by his Name, JESUS.

In I Thessalonians 5:17, the Word of God calls us to pray without ceasing. Consistency in fulfilling this biblical mandate is difficult for us because our minds are constantly charged; we struggle to focus on prayer and to reach that point where we are unaware of time and become lost in the presence of the Lord.

This guide has been prepared to give us that momentum we need. It is not about vain repetitions but intended to be a resource of help when we don't know what to say or how to begin and even times when our souls need help to be drawn into His presence while in prayer.

The beautiful thing is that when we connect with God, our own words will flow naturally without the need to continue reading.

I suggest that if you enjoy praying with music, create a playlist of songs that uplift the Lord Jesus and foster communion with Him, then listen to them during your prayer time. Music originated in heaven for the purpose of praising God. It is natural that when we hear songs that glorify Him, our souls are drawn closer to His Glory.

At the end of this prayer guide, I've included a section where you can document your petitions to God, jot down the names of individuals you want to pray for, and, of course, provide space for personal notes. This will allow you to reference them during your prayer time.

I pray that this prayer guide serves as a tool to connect you with the Presence of our King and Savior, Jesus Christ, and aids in your spiritual growth.

Tere De la Rosa

*I pray that the eyes of your heart may be enlightened
in order that you may know the hope to which*
he has called you,
*the riches of his glorious inheritance
in his holy people.
Ephesians 1:18 (NIV)*

Seek His Face

If my people, which are called by my name, shall humble themselves, and pray, and seek my face, and turn from their wicked ways; then will I hear from heaven, and will forgive their sin, and will heal their land.
2 Chronicles 7:14 (KJV)

- Lord Jesus, I desire to seek Your precious face
- I long for my life to be transformed from glory to glory in Your presence
- Every time I bow down before You, my God, I pray that my humanity be absorbed by Your Divinity
- May Your Light overcome my darkness
- I want to find my identity in You
- Please take hold of my thoughts and my feelings
- Take complete control of my heart
- Dear Lord, if there is any lingering trace of pride within me, I earnestly ask for its complete removal
- My sincere desire is to cultivate humility, as my fervor lies in pleasing you
- I want to be marked and influenced by the beauty of Your Holiness
- May my life be like a tree planted by the stream, bearing the fruit of mercy and justice
- I want to feel Your mighty Presence
- I want to see you

*Open my lips, Lord,
and my mouth will declare your praise.
You do not delight in sacrifice, or I would bring it;
you do not take pleasure in burnt offerings.
My sacrifice, O God, is a broken spirit;
a broken and contrite heart
you, God, will not despise.
Psalm 51: 15-17 (KJV)*

*Test me, Lord, and try me,
examine my heart and my mind.
Psalm 26:2 (NIV)*

Into His Gates

*Enter into his gates with thanksgiving,
and into his courts with praise:
be thankful unto him, and bless his name.
Psalms 100:4 (KJV)*

- Mighty and powerful God, Lord of Hosts, my heart overflows with gratitude for the precious Blood shed on Calvary, securing the forgiveness of my sins
- Thank You for having had mercy on me and for burying my sins into the depths of the sea
- Thank You for Your unconditional, inexhaustible and incomparable love; my life has taken the direction that leads me on the path of your Light
- Thank You for filling me with Your Holy Spirit, who day by day guides me and keeps me firm in Your ways
- Today, I can confidently approach the throne of grace, to attain mercy and find grace in the time of need
- You are my shield, my glory, the One who lifts my head
- My soul praises You
- In Your presence, my heart finds joy

But thou art holy,
O thou that inhabitest the praises of Israel.
Psalms 22:3 (KJV)

They sing the song of Moses, the servant of God,
and the song of the Lamb, saying:

"Great and marvelous are Your works,
Lord God Almighty!
Just and true are Your ways,

O King of the saints!

Who shall not fear You, O Lord, and glorify Your name?
For You alone are holy.
For all nations shall come and worship before You,
For Your judgments have been manifested."
Revelation 15:3-4 (NKJV)

Yours, Lord, is the greatness and the power
and the glory and the majesty and the splendor,
for everything in heaven and earth is yours.
Yours, Lord, is the kingdom;
you are exalted as head over all.
1 Chronicles 29:11 (NIV)

Then we your people, the sheep of your pasture,
will praise you forever;
from generation to generation
we will proclaim your praise..
Psalm 79:13 (NVI)

Shout for joy, you heavens; rejoice, you earth;
burst into song, you mountains!
For the Lord comforts his people
and will have compassion on his afflicted ones.
Isaiah 49:13 (NIV)

Let everything that has breath praise the Lord.
Psalm 150:6 (NIV)

...Hallelujah!

Salvation and glory and power belong to our God,
Revelation 19:1 (NIV)

I praise you because
I am fearfully and wonderfully made;
your works are wonderful,
I know that full well.
Psalms 139:14 (NIV)

Praise be to the Lord my Rock,
who trains my hands for war,
my fingers for battle.
He is my loving God and my fortress,
my stronghold and my deliverer,
my shield, in whom I take refuge...
Psalm 144:1-2 (NIV)

Pray Following The Model Given By The Lord

And it came to pass, that, as he was praying in a certain place, when he ceased, one of his disciples said unto him, Lord, teach us to pray, as John also taught his disciples.
And he said unto them, When ye pray, say:

***Our Father which art in heaven,
Hallowed be thy name.***

Thy kingdom come.

Thy will be done, as in heaven, so in earth.

Give us day by day our daily bread.

And forgive us our sins; for we also forgive every one that is indebted to us.

And lead us not into temptation; but deliver us from evil.

Luke 11:1-4 (KJV)

Our Father which Art In Heaven, Hallowed Be Thy Name

*...But the people that do know their God
shall be strong, and do exploits.
Daniel 11:32 (KJV)*

*Salvation is found in no one else, for there is no other name under
heaven given to mankind
by which we must be saved.
Acts 4:12 (NIV)*

- I exalt, worship and adore your wonderful name Jesus!
- You are my God, my King and Lord
- Your greatness is beyond measure
- You are mighty and awesome
- Doer of wonders; You alone will I praise
- Only before Your divine presence my soul bows down
- All that I am worships before Your Divinity
- Thank You for the revelation of Your Name.
- There is power in Your Name!
- Every knee shall bow and every tongue shall declare that You alone are God
- You alone are worthy, and You alone are holy
- My soul thirsts for you, Prince of Peace

"The Old Testament uses a number of compound names of Jehovah to describe God and to reveal Him further." (David Bernard, The Oneness of God).

If there is something we desire in our prayers, it is a deeper revelation of God. The initial plea in the Lord's Prayer is: "Hallowed be Thy name." When we actively apply this, magnifying, exalting, and bestowing honor upon His mighty Name, declaring His attributes across every aspect of our lives and any crises we may encounter, it sends a message to our souls and wards off the spirits that seek to steal our peace. Regardless of the challenges we face, there is an attribute of God that reassures my soul – He is more than sufficient, covering and protecting me. He is everything I need.

In the upcoming pages, I am utilizing the compilation of compound names of God as outlined by Rev. David Bernard in his book *"The Oneness of God."* Alongside these compound names, I include the corresponding Bible verses provided by Brother Bernard, enabling us to incorporate these divine attributes of our Savior into our prayers, seeking the strength and answers required for any situation we might encounter.

It is crucial to approach our prayers with the understanding that our omniscient, omnipotent, and omnipresent God hears our pleas.

We anticipate the manifestation of His promised glory as we acknowledge the power inherent in His Name.

Jehovah-jireh The Lord will see (i.e., will provide)

And Abraham called the name of that place <u>Jehovahjireh:</u> as it is said to this day, In the mount of the Lord it shall be seen.
Genesis 22:14 (KJV)

Philippians 4:19
But my God shall supply all your need according to his riches in glory by Christ Jesus
Philippians 4:19 (KJV)

- My Lord Jesus, You are my provider
- I trust in You completely
- I am confident that if I strive, following Your guidance, You will bless the fruit of my hands
- I pray that You will grant me the strength and wisdom to work and fulfill my needs
- According to Your Word (Matthew 6:25-34), I should not be anxious about what we will eat or drink, nor worry about the clothes we will wear, because You will provide for each of our needs
- Just as You care for and feed the birds of the air, and clothe the lilies and herbs with beauty, I have faith that, in the same way, You will care for and supply for me and my family
- You know my needs
- My priority and most fervent desire are to seek Your kingdom and righteousness; everything else will be added
- I will not be anxious, for You are with me

- I want to express gratitude for Your provisions
- Help me in discerning the difference between my needs and my wants

---

Write down specific needs for yourself and your family, and present them to Him in prayer, with the assurance that He will provide.

And all things, whatsoever ye shall ask in prayer, believing, ye shall receive.

Matthew 21:22

Jehovah-rapha - The LORD that heals

*He said, "If you listen carefully to the Lord your God and do what is right in his eyes, if you pay attention to his commands and keep all his decrees, I will not bring on you any of the diseases I brought on the Egyptians, **for I am the Lord, who heals you.**"*
Exodus 15:26 (NIV)

- Lord, I begin by praying for the strength to stand firm, attuned to Your voice continually.
- Guide me to walk in righteousness, following Your commandments and keeping Your statutes.
- May Your covenant protection shield me from every ailment.
- If, in any instance, I have faltered, I humbly seek Your forgiveness.
- In accordance with Your unwavering mercy, bring healing to me.
- Extend Your touch to my life, mending my infirmities.
- Heal not only my body but also my mind.

- I repent in Your divine presence, acknowledge my faults, and implore Your forgiveness.
- I want my prayer, whether for myself or others, to be effective.
- According to Your Word, I understand the importance of seeking to be just in Your eyes first.

Take a moment to repent, bringing into the Lord's presence what you know you have done, said, thought, or harbored in your heart that is not pleasing to Him. Wholeheartedly ask Him to remove any root of bitterness from within you that may be hindering your quest to be just before Him.

Is any among you afflicted? let him pray. Is any merry? let him sing psalms. Is any sick among you? let him call for the elders of the church; and let them pray over him, anointing him with oil in the name of the Lord: And the prayer of faith shall save the sick, and the Lord shall raise him up; and if he have committed sins, they shall be forgiven him. Confess your faults one to another, and pray one for another, that ye may be healed.

The effectual fervent prayer of a righteous man availeth much.

James 5:13-16

Jehovah-nissi - The LORD our banner (i.e., victory)

*And Moses built an altar,
and called the name of it <u>Jehovahnissi.</u>
Exodus 17:15 (KJV)*

- As Your Word declares in Psalm 20:5
- I will rejoice in Your salvation
- In Your Name JESUS, I will set up my banners.
- You OH Mighty God, will fulfill all my petitions
- I will not fear, because You are with me
- You will give me *victory* in each one of my battles
- You will never leave me, and will never forsake me

*Thou hast given a banner to them that fear thee,
that it may be displayed because of the truth. Selah.
Psalm 60:4 (KJV)*

*So shall they fear the name of the Lord from the west,
and his glory from the rising of the sun.*
**When the enemy shall come in like a flood,
the Spirit of the Lord shall lift up
a standard against him.**
Isaiah 59:19 (KJV)

Jehovah-m'kaddesh - The LORD that sanctifies

Speak thou also unto the children of Israel, saying, Verily my sabbaths ye shall keep: for it is a sign between me and you throughout your generations;
that ye may know that
__I am the Lord that doth sanctify you.__
Exodus 31:13 (KJV)

- Lord, I pray for Your anointing, Your fresh and liberating oil, to descend from my head to my feet, saturating every part of my being
- I commit my life, my family, and my home to Your service, offering continuous praise and worship unto You

I am the Lord, who brought you up out of Egypt to be your God; therefore be holy, because I am holy.
Leviticus 11:45 (NIV)

- You have delivered me from the bondage of sin
- You are my God
- I pray that You sanctify me
- Cleanse me more and more each day
- I plead Your precious Blood over my life, my home, my spouse and my loved ones

May God himself, the God of peace,
sanctify you through and through.
May your whole spirit, soul and body be kept blameless at the coming of our Lord Jesus Christ.
1 Thessalonians 5:23 (NIV)

Jehovah-shalom - The LORD our peace

Then Gideon built an altar there unto the Lord, and called it <u>Jehovahshalom:</u> unto this day it is yet in Ophrah of the Abiezrites.
Judges 6:24 (KJV)

- I praise You, exalt You, and adore You
- Clinging to and seeking refuge in Your Word, I pray for a peace that surpasses all understanding
- In every circumstance and at all times, I acknowledge that YOU ARE WITH ME!
- I hold onto the promise that You will never leave me nor forsake me
- Your peace breaks every yoke of fear in my life
- I desire to live with the certainty that Your wonderful presence within me will generate the peace my soul longs for
- In moments of uncertainty and despair, I humbly ask You to calm me down. You are my everything

Jehovah-sabaoth - The LORD of hosts (i.e., almighty)

And this man went up out of his city yearly to worship and to sacrifice unto the <u>Lord of hosts</u> in Shiloh...
I Samuel 1:3 (KJV)

- Lord of Hosts, King of Kings, Sovereign God, all honor and majesty to Your Holy Name
- I know that I am surrounded for Your mighty army

Psalm 91:9-12 (NIV)
*If you say, **"The Lord is my refuge,"** and you make the Most High your dwelling, no harm will overtake you, no disaster will come near your tent. For he will command his angels concerning you to guard you in all your ways; they will lift you up in their hands, so that you will not strike your foot against a stone.*

- My family and I need you.
- I implore that a heavenly army surrounds us at all times.
- Help us to always stand firm in your ways, to always be in awe of you, so that Your Presence may always be our shield.

The Lord has established his throne in heaven,
and his kingdom rules over all.
Praise the Lord, you his angels,
you mighty ones who do his bidding,
who obey his word.
Praise the Lord, all his heavenly hosts,
you his servants who do his will.
Praise the Lord, all his works
everywhere in his dominion.
Praise the Lord, my soul.
Psalm 103:19-22 (NIV)

Jehovah-elyon - The LORD most high

*I will praise the Lord according to his righteousness:
and will sing praise to the name of <u>the Lord most high</u>.*
Psalm 7:17 (KJV)

Lift up the name of the Almighty Lord by engaging in the Word of God, vocalizing verses that declare and proclaim His greatness.

I will be glad and rejoice in you;
I will sing the praises of your name, O Most High.
Psalm 9:2 (NIV)

...you alone are the Most High over all the earth.
Psalm 83:18 (NIV)

*It is a good thing to give thanks unto the Lord,
and to sing praises unto thy name, O Most High.*
Psalm 92:1 (KJV)

But thou, Lord, art most high for evermore.
Psalm 92:8 (KJV)

*Who is this King of glory?
The Lord strong and mighty, the Lord mighty in battle.*
Psalm 24:8 (KJV)

*Who is like unto thee, O Lord, among the gods? who is like thee,
glorious in holiness, fearful in praises, doing wonders?*
Exodus 15:11 (KJV)

Hear, O ye kings; give ear, O ye princes; I, even I, will sing unto the Lord; I will sing praise to the Lord God of Israel.
Judges 5:3 (KJV)

Therefore I will give thanks unto thee, O Lord, among the heathen, and I will sing praises unto thy name.
2 Samuel 22:50 (KJV)

For great is the Lord, and greatly to be praised: he also is to be feared above all gods
1 Chronicles 16:25 (KJV)

"Stand up and praise the Lord your God, who is from everlasting to everlasting."
"Blessed be your glorious name, and may it be exalted above all blessing and praise. You alone are the Lord. You made the heavens, even the highest heavens, and all their starry host, the earth and all that is on it, the seas and all that is in them. You give life to everything, and the multitudes of heaven worship you.
Nehemiah 9:5-6 (NIV)

I will bless the Lord at all times:
his praise shall continually be in my mouth.
Psalm 34:1 (KJV)

Great is the Lord, and greatly to be praised in the city of our God, in the mountain of his holiness.
Psalm 48:1 (KJV)

I will praise thee, O Lord my God, with all my heart: and I will glorify thy name for evermore.
Psalm 86:12

Jehovah-raah

The LORD my shepherd

*The Lord is my shepherd, I lack nothing.
He makes me lie down in green pastures,
he leads me beside quiet waters, he refreshes my soul.
He guides me along the right paths for his name's sake.*

*Even though I walk through the darkest valley,
I will fear no evil, for you are with me;
your rod and your staff, they comfort me.*

*You prepare a table before me
in the presence of my enemies.
You anoint my head with oil;
my cup overflows.*

*Surely your goodness and love will follow me
all the days of my life,
and I will dwell in the house of the Lord forever.
Psalm 23 (NIV)*

Jehovah-hoseenu

The LORD our maker

*O come, let us worship and bow down:
let us kneel before the Lord our maker.
Psalm 95:6*

*Know ye that the Lord he is God: it is he that hath made us, and not we ourselves; we are his people, and the sheep of his pasture.
Psalm 100:3*

Thus saith the Lord that made thee, and formed thee from the womb, which will help thee; Fear not, *O Jacob, my servant; and thou, Jesurun, whom I have chosen.*

For I will pour water upon him that is thirsty, and floods upon the dry ground: <u>I will pour my spirit upon thy seed, and my blessing upon thine offspring:</u>

*And they shall spring up as among the grass,
as willows by the water courses.*

Isaiah 44:2-4

Jehovah-Tsidkenu

The Lord is my righteousness

*In his days Judah will be saved
and Israel will live in safety.
This is the name by which he will be called:*
The Lord Our Righteous Savior.
Jeremiah 23:6 (NIV)

- Almighty God, You intervene for Your children who do their very best to please you
- In faith, I clothe myself with the breastplate of righteousness, eliminating the need to fear any injustice perpetrated against me
- You see all things and will defend my cause
- Shape me, Lord, and guide me to act in accordance with Your righteousness, not mine
- I shall not fear, for Your presence is with me
- You are my God, and You will fortify and assist me
- I embrace and claim the promise your promise to uphold me with Your righteous right hand
- You do not overlook any injustice committed against me or my loved ones; therefore, I am confident that you will always defend my cause

Jehovah-shammah
The Lord is present

It was round about eighteen thousand measures: and the name of the city from that day shall be, The Lord is there.
Ezekiel 48:35

Repent ye therefore, and be converted, that your sins may be blotted out, when the times of refreshing shall come from the presence of the Lord.
Acts 3:19

- My Lord and God, there is nothing I desire more in this life than to be assured of Your presence with me
- Your Word affirms that You inhabit in the midst of the praises of Your people. Therefore, with all my heart, I offer my praises, yearning to feel You, O my Lord
- Your presence permeates my surroundings, and I implore You, Lord, to saturate my being
- I love You and need You
- I boldly declare that You are here, present in this very moment
- I firmly believe and confess that, in Your presence, every disturbance must retreat, allowing me to experience the serene peace that Your divine presence brings

Take your time, savor the moment in which you are feeling His Presence. Worship Him.

Selah

More powerful Scriptures To Pray Praising His Name

For unto us a child is born, unto us a son is given: and the government shall be upon his shoulder: and his name shall be called <u>Wonderful, Counsellor, The mighty God, The everlasting Father, The Prince of Peace.</u>
Isaiah 9:6 (KJV)

*She will give birth to a son,
and you are to give him the name Jesus,
because he will save his people from their sins.
All this took place to fulfill what the Lord had said through the prophet: "The virgin will conceive and give birth to a son, and they will call him Immanuel"
(which means "God with us").*
Matthew 1:21-23 (NIV)

*Who will not fear you, Lord,
and bring glory to your name?
<u>For you alone are holy.</u>
All nations will come and worship before you,
for your righteous acts have been revealed.*
Revelation 15:4 (NIV)

*Now, our God, we give you thanks,
and <u>praise your glorious name.</u>*
1 Chronicles 29:13 (NIV)

*<u>But You are holy,
Enthroned in the praises of Israel.</u>*
Psalm 22:3 (NKJV)

*You, Lord, are forgiving and good,
abounding in love to all who call to you.
Psalm 86:5 (NIV)*

*Be exalted, O God, above the heavens;
let your glory be over all the earth.
Psalm 108:5 (NIV)*

*May we shout for joy over your victory
and <u>lift up our banners in the name of our God</u>.
May the Lord grant all your requests.
Now this I know:
The Lord gives victory to his anointed.
He answers him from his heavenly sanctuary
with the victorious power of his right hand.
Some trust in chariots and some in horses,
but we trust in the name of the Lord our God.
They are brought to their knees and fall,
but we rise up and stand firm
Psalm 20:5-8 (NIV)*

Thy Kingdom Come
*(Personalizing Ephesians 3:16-19
and other powerful Scriptures)*

- Lord Jesus, according to the riches of Your glory, I pray that You strengthen me inwardly WITH YOUR POWER BY YOUR SPIRIT and that You may dwell in my heart by faith
- It is my deepest desire to be rooted and grounded in Your love
- I want to be able to comprehend with all the saints how wide and long and high and deep is Your love, which surpasses all knowledge
- I WANT TO BE FILLED WITH ALL YOUR FULLNESS!
- Lord, let me be that house where You can dwell, where You can find rest
- I want to serve You with reverence
- I want to serve You with meekness
- Fill me with Your goodness
- Let Your divine presence flood every corner of my being
- Saturate me
- I declare You King and Lord of my life
- I bow and submit myself to Your divine will
- Have mercy on me, hear my prayer
- Shine upon me the light of Your countenance

- Help me Lord, as 2 Peter 1:5-10 says, to exercise all diligence, adding to my faith virtue, to virtue knowledge, to knowledge self-control, to self-control patience, to patience godliness, to godliness brotherly affection, and to brotherly affection love
- If these things abound in me, I shall not be idle and unfruitful in the knowledge of our Lord Jesus Christ
- I do not want to be short-sighted; I do not want to be blind;
- Let me not forget that You have purified me from my former sins
- I want to make firm my calling and election, for by doing these things I shall never fall
- May Your Kingdom overtake my emotions
- May Your kingdom come into my mind, soul and heart
- May Your Kingdom possess my home
- Take control of all that is happening to my loved ones
- May your Kingdom invade my life
- Do not leave any part of my life unavailable to You
- Take control of my everything, I implore You
- I put in your divine hands that situation that you know worries me
- Lord Jesus, I know that You do not grow weary, but I want to offer You in my heart a place where You can repose
- I want to invite You into the depths of my being

- Enter. Dwell. Possess
- All that I am belongs to You
- I long for You

> *Your throne, O God, will last for ever and ever;*
> *a scepter of justice*
> *will be the scepter of your kingdom.*
> *Psalms 45:6 (NIV)*

> *Your kingdom is an everlasting kingdom,*
> *and your dominion endures through all generations.*
> *The Lord is trustworthy in all he promises*
> *and faithful in all he does*
> *Psalms 145:13 (NIV)*

- In every blessing that is poured out upon my life, You remind me of Your faithfulness
- I declare and believe that am not alone
- You take me by the hand, making me feel safe, even when I walk through the most difficult crossroads
- You hold me

> *I have been crucified with Christ and I no longer live, but Christ lives in me. The life I now live in the body, I live by faith in the Son of God, who loved me and gave himself for me.*
> *Galatians 2:20 (NIV)*

- In the Name of Jesus I declare that it is not my thoughts that dominate me, but the God who lives in me

- It is not my desires that control me, but the perfect will of the One who loves my soul

> *I will speak of the glorious honour of thy majesty,*
> *and of thy wondrous works.*
> *Psalm 145:5 (KJV)*

- My lips declare that You are King of Kings and Lord of lords
- I call upon Your kingdom for my life
- I invoke Your divine Presence
- My soul thirsts for You, the living God
- I cry out to You Lord Jesus
- Rescue me

> *I will worship toward thy holy temple,*
> *and praise thy name*
> *for thy lovingkindness and for thy truth:*
> *for thou hast magnified thy word above all thy name.*
> *Psalms 138:2 (KJV)*

Love the Lord your God with all your heart and with all your soul
and with all your strength.
Deuteronomy 6:5 (NIV)

Thy Will Be Done,
In Earth, As It Is In Heaven

*But as for me, my prayer is unto thee,
O Lord, in an acceptable time:
O God, in the multitude of thy mercy hear me,
in the truth of thy salvation.
Lord, You have a perfect plan for my life;
You have had it since the day that You created me.
Psalm 69:13 (NIV)*

- I pray that nothing outside or inside of me will stand in the way of the fulfillment of Your plan
- May everything that happens in my life and in the lives of my loved ones be according to Your perfect purpose
- May Your will prosper in my hand and in my life
- I do not want to walk in my own ways, nor seek to live following the desires of my flesh and my deceitful heart
- I want to follow You
- I want to yield myself completely to Your perfect will
- Lord, may the influence of Your Holy Spirit within me silence all that offends Your Holiness and love
- I want to walk in Your ways and speak Your words, that I may delight in You, and that You may raise me above the heights of the earth
- Not only do I want to say to You: Lord, Lord, but I want to submit myself entirely to You

- I want the fear of the Lord to be upon me and to live according to Your statutes and commandments
- In my moments of anguish, pain, weakness and worry, many things can go through my mind; I ask You to take full control of any situation and give me divine peace that surpasses my human understanding

If It Be Thy will:

- In my illness, bring healing to me
- Amidst my troubles, grant me serenity
- Through my pain, let the joy of Your salvation console me.
- In moments of sorrow, may I find joy in You
- When burdened, bring calmness to my soul
- In times of affliction, lift my head high
- Amidst bitterness, let me drink from Your sweet spring.
- In weariness, be my source of rest
- When fear invades, may the certainty of Your presence dispel it
- In moments of insecurity, take hold of my hand
- During confusion, be my calm and peace
- Drape my guilt with the embrace of Your forgiveness

The Lord will vindicate me;
your love, Lord, endures forever—
do not abandon the works of your hands.
Psalm 138:8

You have searched me, Lord, and you know me.
You know when I sit and when I rise;
you perceive my thoughts from afar.
You discern my going out and my lying down;
you are familiar with all my ways.
<u>*Before a word is on my tongue*</u>
<u>*you, Lord, know it completely.*</u>
Psalm 139:1-4

I delight to do thy will, O my God: yea,

thy law is within my heart.

Psalm 40:8 (KJV)

Teach me to do your will, for you are my God;
may your good Spirit lead me on level ground.
Psalm 143:10

Make me to go in the path of thy commandments;
for therein do I delight.
Psalm 119:35 (KJV)

Give Us Day By Day Our Daily Bread

The Word of God is your bread, sustenance, support, light, strength and refuge. It is your weapon in battle.
Do not let go of it! Let it cling to your hands and engrave it into your soul.
We must hear it, read it, quote it, use it, live it, learn it and teach it.
It is His Word along with prayer that takes us through the process of sanctification. When we read the Bible with faith and a reverent attitude, it has the power to tame our mind and heart and lead us to moments of intimacy with the Lord Jesus. We are built up spiritually to strengthen our armor which protects us in the constant battle between the flesh and the spirit.

For it is sanctified by the word of God and prayer
I Timothy 4:5 (KJV)

For the word of God is quick, and powerful, and sharper than any twoedged sword, piercing even to the dividing asunder of soul and spirit, and of the joints and marrow, and is a discerner of the thoughts and intents of the heart.
Hebrews 4:12 (KJV)

Finally, be strong in the Lord and in his mighty power.
Put on the full armor of God,
so that you can take your stand against the devil's schemes. For our struggle is not against flesh and blood, but against the rulers, against the authorities, against the powers of this dark world and against the spiritual forces of evil in the heavenly realms. Therefore put on the full armor of God, so that when the day of evil comes, you may be able to stand your ground, and after you have done

everything, to stand. Stand firm then, with the belt of truth buckled around your waist, with the breastplate of righteousness in place, and with your feet fitted with the readiness that comes from the gospel of peace. In addition to all this, take up the shield of faith, with which you can extinguish all the flaming arrows of the evil one. Take the helmet of salvation and the sword of the Spirit, which is the word of God. And pray in the Spirit on all occasions with all kinds of prayers and requests. With this in mind, be alert and always keep on praying for all the Lord's people.
Ephesians 6:10-18 (NIV)

- Lord, sanctify me through Your precious Word
- I pray that Your Word may be the nourishment of my spirit
- Show me my errors and give me the strength to change
- Strengthen my mind
- Establish me in Your ways through Your wonderful precepts
- Guide me on the path of your light, enlightened by Your words
- May Your powerful Word be the protective shield of my mind
- Let not the temptations and afflictions of the world pull me away from You
- Satisfy me with the best of heaven

*Every word of God is pure:
he is a shield unto them that put their trust in him.
Proverbs 30:5 (KJV)*

*And Jesus answered him, saying, It is written,
That man shall not live by bread alone,
but by every word of God.
Luke 4:4 (KJV)*

*He replied, "Blessed rather are those
who hear the word of God and obey it."
Luke 11:28 (NIV)*

*So then faith cometh by hearing, and hearing by the word of God.
Romans 10:17 9 (KJV)*

*But have renounced the hidden things of dishonesty, not walking in
craftiness, nor handling the word of God deceitfully;
but by manifestation of the truth commending ourselves to every
man's conscience in the sight of God.
2 Corinthians 4:2 (KJV)*

- I renounce the desires of my flesh
- I renounce the dead works of my life
- I renounce everything that opposes Your will Lord Jesus

*And take the helmet of salvation, and the sword of the Spirit,
which is the word of God.
Ephesians 6:17 (KJV)*

*The grass withers and the flowers fall,
but the word of our God endures forever.
Isaiah 40:8 (NIV)*

*The words of the Lord are pure words: as silver tried in a furnace of
earth, purified seven times.*

*Thou shalt keep them, O Lord,
thou shalt preserve them from this generation for ever.*
Psalm 12:6-7 (KJV)

- In Your Holy Name Jesus I take the helmet
- I take Your sword
- I cling to Your Word
- You have saved me and I believe it
- I am not weak but I am strong for Your mighty Word is living and active in me
- Within me dwells Your Holy Spirit
- You fill me
- You protect me, and I believe it

*And we also thank God continually for this,
that when you received the word of God
[concerning salvation] which you heard from us,
you welcomed it not as the word of [mere] men,
but as it truly is, the word of God,
which is effectually at work in you who believe [exercising its
inherent, supernatural power
in those of faith].*
1 Thessalonians 2:13 (AMP)

- Lord, let your Word continue to be at work in my life and prosper me, to accomplish what pleases You

*Finally, brethren, pray for us, that the word of the Lord may have
free course, and be glorified,
even as it is with you.
2 Thessalonians 3:1 (KJV)*

*"For as the rain and snow come down from heaven,
And do not return there without watering the earth,
Making it bear and sprout,
And providing seed to the sower and bread to the eater,
So will My word be which goes out of My mouth;
It will not return to Me void (useless, without result),
Without accomplishing what I desire,
And without succeeding in the matter for which I sent it.
Isaiah 55:10-11 (AMP)*

And Forgive Us Our Sins

Come now, and let us reason together, saith the Lord:
though your sins be as scarlet,
they shall be as white as snow;
though they be red like crimson, they shall be as wool.
Isaiah 1:18 (KJV)

- Lord, I come to You
- I lay myself before Your presence
- I confess that I have failed You and I implore You to forgive me

Have mercy on me, O God,
according to Your lovingkindness;
According to the greatness of Your compassion
blot out my transgressions.
Wash me thoroughly from my wickedness and guilt
And cleanse me from my sin.
For I am conscious of my transgressions
and I acknowledge them;
My sin is always before me.
Against You, You only, have I sinned
And done that which is evil in Your sight,
So that You are justified
when You speak [Your sentence]
And faultless in Your judgment.
I was brought forth in [a state of] wickedness;
In sin my mother conceived me
[and from my beginning I, too, was sinful].
Behold, You desire truth in the innermost being,

*And in the hidden part [of my heart]
You will make me know wisdom.
Purify me with hyssop, and I will be clean;
Wash me, and I will be whiter than snow.
Make me hear joy and gladness and be satisfied;
Let the bones which You have broken rejoice.
Hide Your face from my sins
And blot out all my iniquities.
Create in me a clean heart, O God,
And renew a right and steadfast spirit within me.
Do not cast me away from Your presence
And do not take Your Holy Spirit from me.
Restore to me the joy of Your salvation
And sustain me with a willing spirit.
Psalm 51:1-12 (AMP)*

*Search me, O God, and know my heart:
try me, and know my thoughts:
And see if there be any wicked way in me,
and lead me in the way everlasting.
Psalm 139:23-24 (KJV)*

- Lord, I ask You to correct me
- Do not allow hardness to make its nest in my heart
- In the precious Name of the Lord Jesus, I repent for my sins
- Forgive me for everything I have done or thought that goes against Your statutes and commandments
- If in any way I have not been obedient, I ask You to forgive me and reveal it to me, so that with the strength given me by Your Holy Spirit, I may obey You and honor You with my deeds

- Search every part of my being: what I do, what I say, what I feel, what I think. I ask You to be involved even in my dreams
- Whether awake or asleep, may You have control of my entire being
- According to your Word, show me if I walk in the way of wickedness, or if the intentions of my heart are dark
- May Your light, I pray, overcome darkness in me
- Lead me in the way of truth, love, righteousness and holiness
- Lord, forgive me my iniquities
- Forgive my wickedness
- If in the battle between my flesh and my spirit, if in any way I have allowed the flesh to take advantage, I ask You to forgive me and help me to overcome in You
- If I have failed You without knowing it, I also humbly ask You to forgive me
- I surrender my heart to You

For we also Forgive Every one

- Lord, it is easier to ask Your forgiveness for my sins than to forgive those who offend me
- Do not allow any root of bitterness to grow in me
- Help me to forgive all offenses
- Every unjust word against me, I forgive it
- Help me to forgive also those who have offended or hurt my loved ones

Any name that comes to your mind, bring it right now into the presence of the Lord
You will be thinking that you cannot say you have forgiven because you do not yet feel it
Confess with your lips, in the presence of God, your desire to forgive and let the Lord do the work in you

- Lord, I recognize the condition of my heart and admit before your presence that I have not yet forgiven: (*the name of the person who offended you*)
- For having: (*the offense*)
- I expose myself before You and implore for Your consuming fire to burn those feelings that destroy me and displease You

- In Your Holy Name Jesus, I forgive him/her and I pray that you help me to get past the offense and not allow bitterness to take root neither in my mind nor in my heart

And Lead Us Not Into Temptation

*Watch and pray, that ye enter not into temptation:
the spirit indeed is willing, but the flesh is weak.
Matthew 26:41 (KJV)*

*No temptation [regardless of its source] has overtaken or enticed you that is not common to human experience [nor is any temptation unusual or beyond human resistance]; but God is faithful [to His word—He is compassionate and trustworthy], and He will not let you be tempted beyond your ability [to resist],
but along with the temptation He [has in the past and is now and] will [always] provide the way out as well, so that you will be able to endure it [without yielding, and will overcome temptation with joy].
1 Corinthians 10:13 (AMP)*

- Lord Jesus, only by holding Your hand, rooted in Your Word and in Your divine presence can I find that door of escape that You provide for me
- Whenever I am tempted, it is only by abiding in You that I can stand strong
- In any situation that comes my way, where my flesh wants to take control, I ask that Your Divinity overcome my humanity
- I submit my life entirely to You in prayer

- Give me the wisdom, which is the fear of the Lord, to flee from any situation in which my flesh is exposed to cruel temptation

> *No weapon that is formed against thee shall prosper;*
> *and every tongue that shall rise against thee in judgment thou shalt condemn.*
> *This is the heritage of the servants of the Lord,*
> *and their righteousness is of me, saith the Lord.*
> *Isaiah 54:17 (KJV)*

But Deliver Us From Evil

> *Keep your servant also from willful sins;*
> *may they not rule over me. Then I will be blameless,*
> *innocent of great transgression.*
> *May these words of my mouth*
> *and this meditation of my heart*
> *be pleasing in your sight,*
> *Lord, my Rock and my Redeemer.*
> *Psalm 19:13-14 (NIV)*

> *II lift up my eyes to the mountains—*
> *where does my help come from?*
> *My help comes from the Lord,*
> *the Maker of heaven and earth.*
> *He will not let your foot slip—*
> *he who watches over you will not slumber.*
> *Psalm 121:1-3 (NIV)*

- Lord, I ask for divine protection for my life and the lives of all those I love
- I pray that an army of angels will encamp around us at all times
- Lord, deliver us from any harm that has been planned for our lives
- Frustrate the plans of the enemy
- Let no weapon forged against me or my loved ones prosper
- Salvation comes from You, I pray Your blessing descend upon us

> *It is God who arms me with strength*
> *and keeps my way secure.*
> *He makes my feet like the feet of a deer;*
> *he causes me to stand on the heights.*
> *Psalm 18:32-33 (NIV)*

- Lord Jesus, Glorious Father, give me the spirit of wisdom and revelation
- Enlighten the eyes of my understanding to know the hope to which You have called me

Pray With Songs And Psalms

The Lord is my strength and song, and he is become my salvation: he is my God, and I will prepare him an habitation; my father's God, and I will exalt him.
Exodus 15:2 (KJV)

I have extracted prayers from the beautiful songs and psalms found in the Word of God; in some parts, I have personalized them

From The Song Of Moses And Miriam: (Exodus 15)

- I will sing to the LORD, for he is highly exalted
- The LORD is my strength and my song. He is my defense and my salvation
- He is my God, and I will praise Him
- The LORD is a Mighty Warrior
- Your right hand, O LORD, is magnified in power
- Who among the gods is like You, O LORD?
- Who is like You, O Jehovah, magnificent in holiness, awesome in glory, working wonders?
- You in your unfailing love will lead the people you have redeemed
- In Your strength you will guide me to Your holy dwelling

- You will bring me in and plant me on the mountain of Your inheritance- the place, Lord, You made for Your dwelling, the sanctuary, Lord, Your hands established
- The LORD will reign forever and ever
- I sing to You, O LORD, because you are highly exalted, for you have magnified yourself exceedingly!

From The Song Of Moses (Deuteronomy 32)

- I will proclaim Your name, O LORD
- Your are my Rock, Your work is perfect
- All Your ways are uprightness
- God of truth and without iniquity
- Righteous and upright!
- YOU ARE MY CREATOR
- You have made me and established me
- You found me in a desert land and in a wilderness of horrible loneliness
- Your have instructed me and kept me as the apple of your eye
- Hide not your face from me
- YOU ARE THE GREAT I AM
- I ask You for life, I ask You for healing

From The Song Of Deborah And Barak (Judges 5)

- I will sing psalms to the LORD, the God of Israel

- I come before You Lord with resolutions in my heart
- I come before You Lord with purpose in my heart
- As Deborah declared, so I declare that from the heavens the stars shall fight for me
- March, O my soul, with power

From The Song Of Hannah (1 Samuel 2)

- My heart rejoices in the LORD
- My power is exalted in the LORD
- My mouth is enlarged in my trials
- I rejoice in Your salvation, O God
- There is none Holy like You
- There is none beside You
- And there is no refuge You
- The God of all knowledge is Jehovah
- And to Him is the weighing of deeds
- The LORD kills and gives life
- He brings down to Sheol, and brings up
- The Lord sends poverty and wealth;
- He humbles and He exalts
- He raises the poor from the dust
- The pillars of the earth are the LORD'S, And He establishes the world upon them
- He will guard the feet of His faithful servants
- No man shall be strong by His own strength
- The LORD exalts the strength of His Anointed

From David's Song Of Deliverance (2 Samuel 22)

- The LORD is my rock and my fortress, and my deliverer
- My God, my strength, in Him will I trust
- My shield, and the fortress of my salvation
- I will call upon the LORD, who is worthy to be praised
- In my distress I called upon the LORD, and cried unto my God
- He heard my voice from His temple, and my clamor has reached His ears
- Cleanse my hands, O Lord; I desire to keep Your ways
- I will not stray wickedly from You
- All Your decrees are before me
- I will not depart from Your statutes
- I want to be upright before You
- Keep me from my iniquity
- For You save the afflicted people
- You are my lamp, O LORD: my God will lighten my darkness
- With You will I break down armies, and with my God will I break down walls
- As for God, His way is perfect, and the Word of the LORD is perfect
- He is a shield to all who hope in Him
- For who is God but the LORD alone?
- And what rock is there besides our God?
- God is He who strengthens me

- And who clears my way
- Who makes my feet like hinds' feet
- And makes me firm upon my high places
- He prepares my hands for battle
- You have also given me the shield of your salvation
- You have enlarged my steps under me, and my feet have not slipped
- You have girded me with strength for the battle
- Blessed be my Rock; and the God of my salvation be exalted

From Psalm 28

- I will cry unto You, O LORD
- You are my Rock, do not turn away from me, lest I be like those who go down to the grave, leaving me behind
- Hear the voice of my supplications when I cry unto You. When I lift up my hands unto Your holy temple
- Blessed be the LORD, who has heard the voice of my supplications
- Lord Jesus, you are my strength and my shield, my heart trusted in You, and I was helped, so that my heart rejoiced, I PRAISE YOU WITH MY SONG
- You Lord, are the strength of Your people, And the saving refuge of your anointed
- Save Your people, and bless Your inheritance; and shepherd them, and sustain them for evermore

From Psalm 32

- I have declared my sin unto You, and have not covered mine iniquity
- I said, I will confess my transgressions unto You LORD; and You forgave the iniquity of my sin. Selah
- For this shall every saint pray unto You in the time when You may be found
- You are my refuge; You shall keep me from trouble: You shall compass me about with songs of deliverance. Selah

- Make me to understand, teach me the way in which I should walk
- My hope is in You
- Surround me with Your mercy
- Many sorrows shall be to the wicked: but he that waiteth upon the LORD, mercy shall compass him about
- Rejoice in the LORD and be glad
- Sing for joy, all you upright in heart

From Psalm 34

- I will bless the LORD at all times; His praise shall continually be in my mouth
- I will glory in the Lord
- I glorify and exalt His name
- I sought the Lord, and He answered me; He delivered me from all my fears
- Those who look to Him are radiant; their faces are never covered with shame
- You always save me out of all my troubles
- I believe and declare that the angel of the Lord encamps around those who fear Him and He delivers them
- Taste and see that the Lord is good; blessed is the one who takes refuge in Him
- Oh Lord, I TAKE REFUGE IN YOU
- It is my desire to keep my tongue from evil and my lips from telling lies

- Help me my dear God, to always turn from evil and do good
- *Help me to seek peace and pursue it*
- I want Your eyes to be on me and Your ears attentive to my cry
- Your word says that the righteous cry out, and You hear them and deliver them from all their troubles
- You are close to the brokenhearted and save those who are crushed in spirit
- Lord I know that You rescue your servants; here I am save me from all my afflictions, from every attack and from any mental oppression
- I take my refuge in You and know that I won't be condemned

Who among the gods is like you, Lord?
Who is like you—majestic in holiness,
awesome in glory, working wonders?
Exodus 15:11 (NIV)

*And they sang together by course in praising and giving thanks unto
the Lord; because he is good,
for his mercy endureth for ever toward Israel.
And all the people shouted with a great shout,
when they praised the Lord, because the foundation of the house of
the Lord was laid.
Ezra 3:11 (KJV)*

The heavens declare the glory of God;

*the skies proclaim the work of his hands.
Psalm 19:1*

*Lift up your heads, you gates;
be lifted up, you ancient doors,
that the King of glory may come in.
Who is this King of glory?
The Lord strong and mighty,
the Lord mighty in battle.
Lift up your heads, you gates;
lift them up, you ancient doors,
that the King of glory may come in.
Who is he, this King of glory?
The Lord Almighty—he is the King of glory.
Psalm 24:7-10 (NIV)*

*Be exalted, O God, above the heavens;
let your glory be over all the earth.
Psalm 57:11 (NIV)*

*And blessed be his glorious name for ever:
and let the whole earth be filled with his glory;
Amen, and Amen.
Psalm 72:19 (KJV)*

*In the year that King Uzziah died,
I saw the Lord, high and exalted, seated on a throne;
and the train of his robe filled the temple.
Above him were seraphim, each with six wings:
With two wings they covered their faces,
with two they covered their feet,
and with two they were flying.
And they were calling to one another:*
**"Holy, holy, holy is the Lord Almighty;
the whole earth is full of his glory."**
*At the sound of their voices the doorposts and thresholds shook and
the temple was filled with smoke.
Isaiah 6:1-4 (NIV)*

*And the glory of the Lord will be revealed,
and all people will see it together.
For the mouth of the Lord has spoken.
Isaiah 40:5 (NIV)*

*For the earth shall be filled
with the knowledge of the glory of the Lord,
as the waters cover the sea.
Habakkuk 2:14 (NIV)*

*And the Lord shall be king over all the earth:
in that day shall there be one Lord,*

and his name one.

Zechariah 14:9 (NIV)

To order visit:
www.teredelarosa.com

www.ingramcontent.com/pod-product-compliance
Lightning Source LLC
Chambersburg PA
CBHW051702090426
42736CB00013B/2504